Daphne Burgess

A KING AMONGST TOYS

The Miniature Pinscher

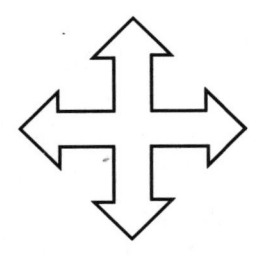

Published By Onyx

ISBN 0 9536790 0 4

Copyright ,, Daphne Burgess 1999

No part of this book may be reproduced or transmitted in any form or by any means, electronic or mechanical, including photocopying, recording, or by any information storage and retrieval system, without permission in writing from the publisher.

ACKNOWLEDGMENTS

NYLABONE, for their help and information.
The word Nylabone is a registered trade mark.

Charles Morgan 'Snaffles', for his help and
Co-operation.

The Kennel Club. Illustrated breed standard
Reproduced by kind permission of 'The Kennel Club,
And illustrated by Sonya Saxby.

ISBN 0 9536790 0 4

Printed and bound in the UK by,
Cheshire County Press Ltd,
England

Published by Onyx,
Congleton,
Cheshire,
England

CONTENTS

To show or not to show

Feeding and Nutrition

Toilet Training

Breeding

The loyal friend

Miniature Pinscher Illustrated Breed Standard Reproduced by kind permission of The Kennel Club and Illustrated by Sonya Saxby

Putting on the style

Crufts 1999

For Susan.

*Whose persistence and Pressurising
got me started. With gentle persuasion, she cajoled, pleaded,
pushed and finally persuaded me to write this book.
I hope you like it Sue.*

1

A KING AMONGST TOYS

Of all the small dogs around today, none can be more enchanting than the Miniature Pinscher or Min Pin as these tiny creatures are affectionately called. It is no wonder that they have been given the title, "The King of Toys".

They originate from Germany, where they have been around for hundreds of years. People wrongly assume them to be a direct descendant of the Doberman, but this is not so, although they resemble the Doberman in miniature a great deal.

It is believed that the Miniature Pinscher evolved from the ancient German Pinscher family of dogs, which ultimately produced a number of the breeds, recognised by the Kennel Club today. In 1836 Dr H G Rinchenbach, a German writer stated: "The Miniature Pinscher is a cross of the Dachshund and the Italian Greyhound."

Historians and those who have researched the background of the breed now generally accept this conclusion of Dr Rinchenbach. In any event, Germany is undisputed as the home of origin, where the Miniature Pinscher was known as the "Reh Pinscher" due to its resemblance to a small red deer, the Reh, which freely roamed the German forests many years ago.

It was Louis Doberman who bred his first miniature Pinscher in 1890, and they have been in this country now for over fifty years. They are a unique breed, and one which is becoming increasingly popular in this country as well as in the United States.

If you are tempted to rush out and purchase a Min Pin, think again. They are not a breed of dog one should consider lightly. Anyone who knows anything about this delightful canine will tell you, they are in a class of their own, giving and demanding, a lot of attention. The Min Pin is not suited to everyone. For example: families with very young children would do well to think twice before bringing such a lively little dog into their home. A very young child cannot possibly appreciate nor understand the needs of a Miniature Pinscher, especially a puppy, which will require almost if not more attention than a child itself. Not only that, a Min Pin as a young pup is incredibly small.

Children are not always careful, running around the house, they could quite easily tread on the tiny dog, and cause it serious harm. It is therefore considered being in the interests of both puppy and owner if the young Min Pin goes to a home where it is cared for with the same gentle tenderness one would give to a new born babe.

This is not to say children and Min Pins cannot live together. Of course they can. In the correct environment and with the utmost care, the two go together really well. Provided you make your children understand that Min Pins are not something they can treat disrespectfully, they will grow up to love and respect the newcomer which will bring so much joy to all concerned, the effort is well worthwhile.

Miniature Pinschers require so much of your time. They definitely would not be suited to someone who is out at work all day. Such an action would be cruel to say the least. Min Pins are attention seekers. Their world is full of excitement, and to these endearing little dogs, every moment is filled with wonder.

Min Pins need company, and it would be both cruel and unwise to leave them alone for very long periods.

The Miniature Pinscher basically comes in three colours, Red, Black and Tan and Chocolate and Tan, Chocolate being the rarer of the three. However, it is worth noting that should you want to buy one, you should not be expected to pay any more for a Chocolate and Tan than you would one of the other two colours. There are many breeders of Miniature Pinschers, and you should not buy from anyone who is not registered with the Kennel Club, or indeed recognised by The Miniature Pinscher Club.

Buy from a reputable breeder, and make sure you see the puppy with its mother before you buy. This will give you some indication as to the dogs character, and believe you me, they do have character.

I would not describe a Min Pin as a tidy dog. Tidy in appearance yes, but in nature, that is a totally different matter. They can be excitable, noisy, destructive and at times stubborn. These are obstacles which can be overcome with a lot of patience. However, do not make the mistake that you can change a Min Pin to suit your needs, their needs must always come first. These busy little dogs, I can think of no other way to describe them for they are perpetually on the go, will however bring you a lot of pleasure. They will greet you by jumping up at you, paws scratching, their little stump of a tail wagging, and their tiny bodies all a quiver.

Play is essential to their well being, and they need plenty of toys. It is almost like having a baby in the family, such is their demand for attention.

The Miniature Pinscher is not regarded as an outdoor dog, It would be unwise to expect any Min Pin to have to spend long hours shut up in an outside kennel, especially during the colder months. In fact when they are taken out, a coat is needed to protect them from the elements during the winter or cold weather. A very young puppy can be kept warm by the use of an old woollen sock. Cut off one end, make four holes for the legs, and sew around the raw edges. The same can be made from the sleeve of a woollen jumper, cutting it to the length required. Measure the length of the puppy's back, then cut that amount from the sleeve starting at the cuff.

It will not be an easy task. I have never known any Min Pin to stay still for very long. If your wardrobe does not contain a suitable jumper for cutting up, do not despair. A trip to your local charity shop could well solve the problem. Not only will you be giving your puppy the protection he/she needs, but you have the added benefit of knowing your purchase will also be giving money to a good cause, and your puppy can be kept warm for just a few pounds.

You may think you are the master or mistress, but your little Min Pin will show you otherwise. It is they who will be in control, pleading with you to take notice, to comfort and to play with them. I have been in the company of Min Pins who have quite worn me out. They are not a dog you can ignore. It is no good expecting that once you have fed them, perhaps taken them for a short walk, that they will then settle down. Nothing could be father from the truth. Being a small dog, they do not require very long walks, but once they have had a brief nap, they are up and about, and raring to go. Out come the toys, which for a Min Pin must be plentiful. Not only that the toys must be safe.

Any reputable pet store will advise you as to the type of toys suitable for such a small and agile dog. One toy which I have found to be a firm favourite with Min Pins is the cotton bone. This consists of strands of bright coloured cotton, thickly plaited and knotted securely at each end. The overall shape very much resembles a bone. They come in several sizes, and there is sure to be one, which is just right, whatever the size and age of your dog.

Another thing to remember are the hazards your dog could face just in the home. Make sure that all electrical wiring is kept well out of their reach, and check for sharp corners on furniture or any protruding objects which could cause injuries should they run into them. It is a good idea to take yourself down to their level. Crawl around the floor.

If you come across something low down which looks dangerous, then it probably is, and steps should be taken to improve the situation. Balloons, elastic bands, plastic and items such as sewing thread or

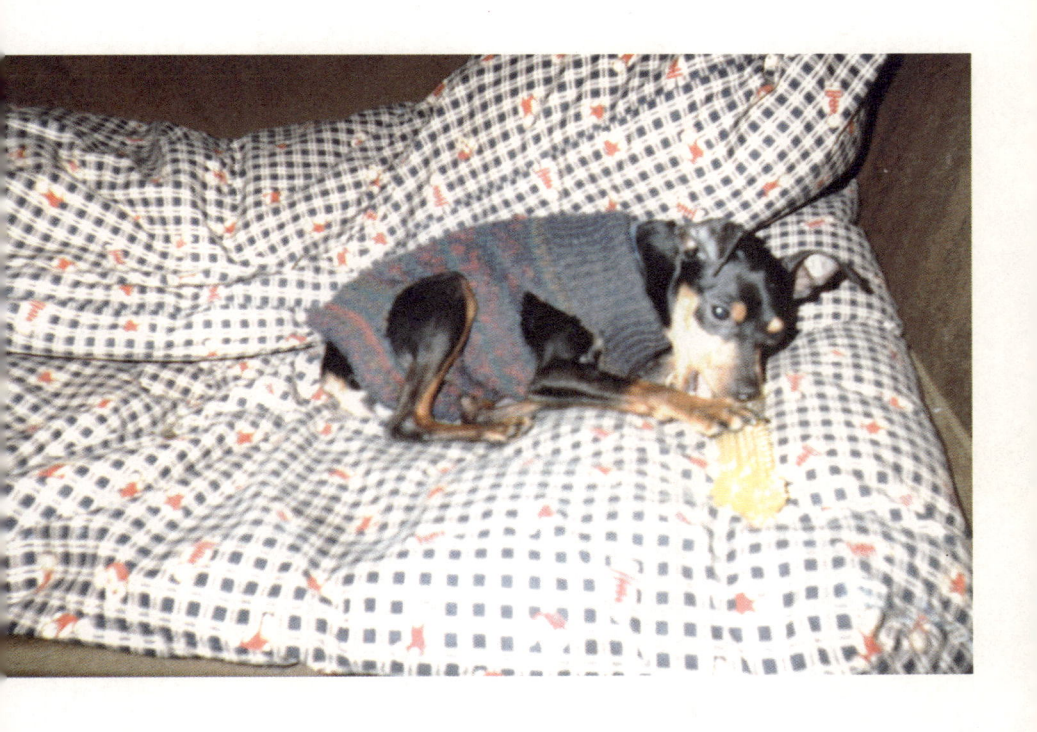

This puppy is wearing a coat made from the sleeve of an old woollen jumper.

knitting wool, if left lying about could soon be swallowed up by inquisitive jaws. If such a thing did happen, the consequences could be serious.

Many houseplants, and garden ones too for that matter, are poisonous to Min Pins. Here is a selection of the most popular ones: *Ivy, Cyclamen, the Daffodil, Delphinium, Poinsettia,* and *Foxglove* to name but a few. If you are uncertain about any plant in your house or garden, the veterinary surgeon will be only too happy to advise you.

Most people know that rhubarb leaves are poisonous, both to animals and humans, but not every one is aware that rhubarb leaves can be fatal if chewed or swallowed. Another source of poison for all dogs is chocolate. Never feed your dog chocolate, no matter how small an amount. Chocolate prepared for human consumption contains theobromine, a bitter white alkaloid which is obtained from the cacao seed, and related to caffeine. The chocolate dog treats which one buys from pet shops or supermarkets are free of this substance, and therefore completely safe for your dog.

Every Min Pin sold should come with this tag: **HANDLE WITH CARE**. Few people realise just how much care a Min Pin needs. You must treat this little dog in the same way you would treat a baby or small child, both are precious.

If you really have your heart set on owning a Miniature Pinscher, and feel able to cope with all the demands of this special breed, but have doubts about your ability to take one into your home, then may I suggest the following;

Seek out other Min Pin owners. If possible ask to spend some time with them so that you can get to know their pets. Many Min Pins may look alike, but in character they will be completely different. Visit as many shows as you can where you can view the Min Pin in a different environment. Take note of the bond between pet and owner. Ask yourself if you feel confident that you can give as much of yourself as this toy dog, King in its own right, will beg of you.

Everyone has a soft spot for a Min Pin, and the older child is no exception. They will be captivated by the charm of this little dog, and provided they are made aware of all the dogs requirements, taught how to treat and respect the new member of the family, then everything will be fine.

There is still much more to owning a Min Pin, and in the following pages, advice is given on everything from personal care to protecting the little one, keeping him or her safe and well, happy and contented.

IVY

CYCLAMEN

POINSETTIA

DAFFODIL

DELPHINIUM

FOXGLOVE

Some of the plants, which are poisonous to Miniature Pinschers.

2

TO SHOW OR NOT TO SHOW

Let us assume you are now the proud owner of a Miniature Pinscher. In no time at all you will wonder how you ever survived without this cute little friend. Indeed it would not surprise me if you are not already thinking of owning a second dog. Most Min Pin owners confess, one of these animals is never enough.

Your puppy should have been vaccinated between six and eight weeks old. The second vaccination at ten to twelve weeks, followed by a booster once a year. This is necessary to protect against potentially fatal and dangerous diseases, such as:

DISTEMPER: Which is also known as Hardpad, and still common. The symptoms are runny nose and eyes.

PARAINFLUENZA: A virus which causes a respiratory disease in the kennel cough syndrome. Though not usually fatal or serious it causes an irritating cough, which is unpleasant, and can be dangerous in an older dog.

PARVOVIRUS: A nasty and relatively new disease having entered this

Country in 1979. In most dogs it causes an acute haemorrhage (bloody) gastro-enteritis, which can cause death within 24 hours.

LEPTOSPIROSIS: Which is two diseases caused by two very closely related bacteria, one of which affects the liver and the other the kidneys.

ADENOVIRUS 2: A virus which again causes a respiratory disease in the kennel cough syndrome.

HEPATITIS: A virus which causes inflammation of the liver.

Besides being vaccinated, your puppy should have had its tail docked and dew-claws removed no later than three days old. The docking of the tail, and the removal of dew claws must be done by a qualified veterinary surgeon. It is illegal for anyone other than a vet to carry out this operation. The ears of the British Miniature Pinscher are not cropped.

The docking of the tail, is not done for medical reasons, it is purely for show as it enhances the appearance of the dog. There are some Min Pin owners who prefer to keep their dog's tail as nature intended it. Now we come to the question of worming. Your puppy will have been wormed by the breeder. However there may well be immature worms in the body tissues, and these can infest the gut just the same.

There are two kinds of worms in all breeds of dog in this country. These are tapeworms and roundworms. Of roundworms, nearly all puppies are infected at birth. Puppies should be wormed at least twice up to six months of age. Adult dogs should be wormed once every six months.

Tapeworms are somewhat different in that they are not passed on from dog to dog. They are caused by the infection of fleas which can pass this particular type of worm to your dog. If your dog has fleas, the tapeworm can be detected in its motions. A course of worming tablets will soon correct the situation.

The Kennel Club will expect you to show your Miniature Pinscher. After all, who would want to hide away such an excellent creature. However, not all Min Pins are born perfect. Some may have a defect in shape or size. Perhaps their colouring is miss matched. White on the chest of a Black and Tan is undesirable as far as judging goes. This would not disqualify a dog, and a small patch of white fur which can be covered by a thumb is acceptable. Never the less, those not suitable for showing still make excellent pets, but it would be advisable to have the dog neutered in order to prevent the unfortunate flaws from being passed on.

Registration with the Kennel Club is essential if you wish to show your dog. The Kennel Club address is given at the back of this book.

Once registered, you will be kept informed as to the dates and venues of dog shows. all over the country.

A copy of the Kennel Club breeding standards is included in a later chapter. All puppies brought from a breeder should have vaccination certificates and these should be passed on to you. If you are intending to show, do not buy any puppy which is offered for sale without the necessary pedigree papers. A puppy which cowers away in corners, has runny eyes or is obviously suffering some form of illness should be avoided.

When you bring your puppy home for the first time you will want to know how to care for it now that it has been taken away from its mother, and perhaps brothers and sisters. He or she will be feeling very insecure, and probably very stressful. Place the puppy in a suitable bed at night. A cardboard box will do to begin with. Cut a part of one side away, this will enable your Min Pin to get in and out easily. A baby's hot water bottle filled with hand-hot water, and wrapped in a blanket should be placed under a layer of bedding to keep the puppy warm.

Remember he or she will be missing their mother's comfort. A loud ticking alarm clock under several layers will give your Min Pin the security of a simulated heart beat which he or she would have associated

Besides being too tall for showing, this Black and Tan Dog has a white mark on his chest, which sadly makes him undesirable.

with the dam. As your Min Pin becomes familiar with its new surroundings and is no longer showing signs of stress, the bottle and alarm clock can be done away with.

The puppy being so small could quite easily be trodden on accidentally, and a serious injury could be the result. To avoid the danger of having this happen place your puppy in a safe container. There are pens available, rather like a child's play pen in which you can place the pup while you are going about your household chores should it happen to be in the same room. This is also advisable if you have children running about at home. These pens are commonly called X pens by a number of people. Any good pet shop should stock the type of pen you require.

A Min Pin intended for showing should be crated. Begin by placing a blanket together with a toy or two inside a cage or carrier. Leave the door open so that he/she may wander in and out as they please. This will get your dog used to the idea of being in a cage. A process which is necessary when transporting to shows. When your Min Pin seems confident about spending time inside the cage, shut the door, extending the time of closure gradually. In this way you should have no trouble getting your Min Pin into a cage when the time comes. This procedure will reduce stress, both for you, and your dog.

A play pen will keep your new puppy safe, and out of harm's way.

There are a number of various cages on the market, and it is worth buying a good quality one. You want nothing but the best for your dog. If all this seems daunting, relax you are not alone. Other new Min Pin owners have been through the same problems, and it is reassuring to know that there is help every step of the way.

There is a Miniature Pinscher Club in Great Britain. The Club secretary is Mr A. Saxby. He and his wife Sonya also own Miniature Pinschers, as well as giving their time to border Collie rescue. Sonya also runs the Miniature Pinscher Club shop, where it is possible to purchase anything from Min Pin stickers for your car, to other decorative and more valuable items, all with Min Pins in mind.

Membership to the club costs just a few pounds, and the information you will receive is worth every penny. You will find Sonya Saxby most helpful. She will answer your queries, giving you help and advice whenever needed. The club also sends out regular news letters.
The Miniature Pinscher Club in Great Britain was formed in 1963, and has almost 200 members. Three shows are held each year. One in the North of the country, one Central and one in the South. Whether you intend to show your Miniature Pinscher or not, membership to the Miniature Pinscher Club is recommended. To become a member, simply write to: *Mr Alan Saxby (Hon Secretary) 39, Nethergate Stannington, Nr. SHEFFIELD, South Yorkshire. S66 DH. Or Telephone: (0114 233 3467.*

Older children and Miniature Pinschers get along together very well

3

FEEDING AND NUTRITION

It is not enough just to feed your dog. He or she must be given the right kind of food. What is correct for an older dog will certainly be unsuitable for a tiny puppy. The breeder from whom you purchased your Min Pin will be able to advise you as they will have already started the puppy off on a suitable diet. If you are unsure about feeding habits, remember your puppy has only got a small stomach so small amounts of food should be given. About three or four small meals a day is recommended until your puppy is about eight months old. It is worth noting that a lot of Miniature Pinscher owners feed their animals on dried food. This is because it is more convenient, also dried dog food actually cause less tartar on the teeth. If you wish to try giving your dog dried food it can be made more palatable by adding a small amount of warm boiled water. It goes without saying that your dog must have access to fresh drinking water at all times.

Later on you can introduce small pieces of chopped chicken or tripe. I do not advise giving your dog pork as it can play havoc with their digestive system and can even cause severe diarrhoea.

Never give your dog chicken bones. They easily splinter, and if a piece of chicken bone was accidentally swallowed, no matter how small, it could quite easily puncture their insides. In fact to be on the safe side, it would be better if you did not give your dog any bones at all.

There is a firm called NYLABONE, and once your dog has been weaned, you will find Nylabone products invaluable. The word `Nylabone` is a registered trademark, and the firm has been manufacturing dog bones for the past 40 years. They specialise in making edible and chewable bones for dogs. Your little Min Pin can get his or her teeth into a Nylabone edible which has all the following advantages. They are healthy, safe, sterilised and highly palatable with no added salt or sugar, and are completely free from artificial colours, and flavours. They also contain no preservatives.

The range is as follows:
Carrot Bone, made up of minced carrots and milk protein moulded into a hard bone shape.
Chooz, made of sterilised chicken meal and milk protein. Chooz can also be cooked in a microwave to produce a softer crunchy texture.
POPpups. These are made from potato starch and natural meat, moulded into a hard bone. They are healthy and dogs love them.
POPpups can also be cooked in a microwave to turn them into a larger

27

28

crunchy treat.

Roar-Hide is made from rawhide which has been minced and moulded into a hard bone. Because the rawhide has been minced any lumps swallowed simply break down into small pieces and do not swell up like some other rawhide .Roar-Hide is moulded at high temperatures and is bacteriologically safe. It is clean and hygienic in use.

The Nylabones made for chewing actually help take care of your dog's teeth. This is because when the bone is being chewed it is raked up into small "bristles" which have the effect of helping to control the deposit of tartar on dog's teeth. The small "bristles" that are worn off the Nylabone are totally harmless, dogs cannot chew off large pieces.

There is a Nylabone for puppies called Puppybone. It is a little softer than Nylabone and has been designed for young dogs. It is recommended that Puppybone is not given to dogs over six months old because older dogs can wear it away more quickly. Puppybone comes in three sizes. There is also a petite Nylabone for very small dogs so your Min Pin has plenty of choice.

All Nylabones can be washed boiled or sterilised as required, and should you find you have not made the correct choice of Nylabone for your dog don't worry, Nylabone will change it at no extra cost for a more suitable product.

Besides the chews and edible bones, Nylabone also make a product called dental floss, the dental floss exerciser is perfectly safe and can be washed boiled or sterilised. No doubt Nylabone will continue the good work of providing safe and effective products for all dogs for many years to come.

It is essential that all food and water bowls used by your Min Pin should be kept scrupulously clean.

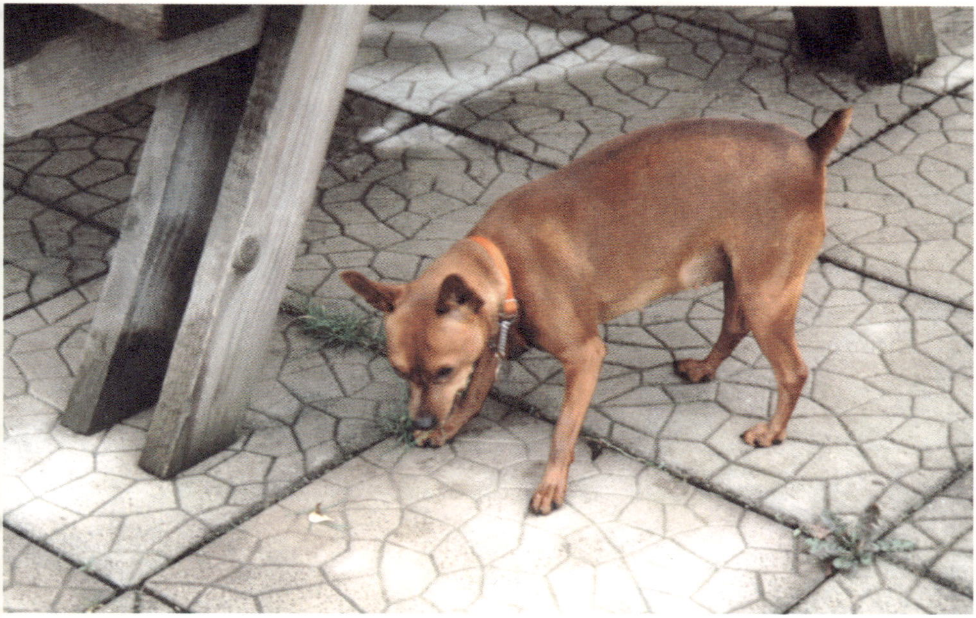

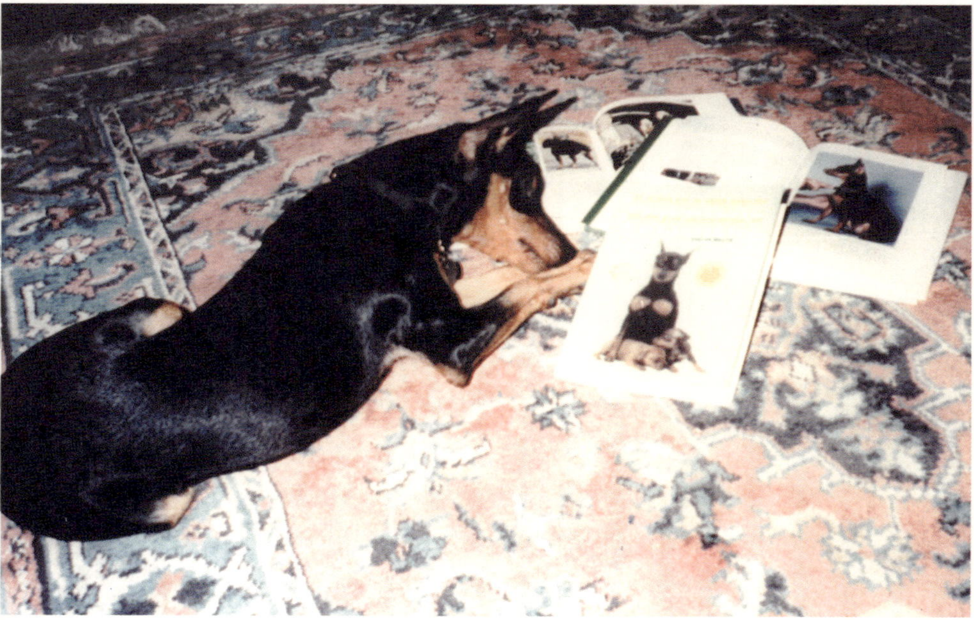

4

TOILET TRAINING

Your new Min Pin may have already had some basic house training by its breeder. If this is not the case, remember a puppy needs to empty its bladder about six times a day, and it is up to you to let him or her know where this action can take place.

House training should begin the moment you bring your puppy home. After meals, take your Min Pin outside so that it may relieve itself. Always give praise to your puppy when this is done as it will encourage them to perform their natural functions in a place where it is acceptable. If you use a phrase like "be clean" when the puppy relieves itself, it will associate the words "be clean" with what it must do. On occasions when the weather is too bad to allow your dog outside, the words "be clean" can be used to persuade the puppy to make use of a sheet of newspaper for its toiletry.

Given a short command repeatedly will imprint on the dog's mind what it must do. Eventually when your puppy hears the words "be clean", he or she will know what you are asking of it. This practice comes in very handy when visiting unfamiliar places. It is possible to train your puppy to use a cat litter tray. Lined with newspaper, it is ideal for flat dwellers or for those unexpected times when the weather or other circumstances prevent you from taking your puppy outside. Keep the litter tray well away from where the dog eats or sleeps. When changing the newspaper, bring the bottom sheet to the top. This is so that the dog can smell its scent, reinforcing the message that this and no where else in the house is the place for performing its natural functions.

On no account should you use bleach on areas in the home where your dog has access. Bleach contains ammonia, and the smell will excite him or her to urinate in places you would not welcome.

There are a number of excellent cleaners for use on kitchen floors, and you are sure to find one which suits both you and your new Min Pin.

When out and about with your Miniature Pinscher, always remember to take a poop scoop with you. Cleaning up after your dog is your responsibility, and no one else's.

5

GROOMING AND HEALTH CARE

Miniature Pinschers have a short hair coat which requires the minimum of care. Begin by briskly rubbing down the coat with your finger tip. This will loosen any dead skin. The next step is to brush the coat thoroughly with a natural bristle brush. A chamois leather can be used to rub down the coat giving it a healthy shine.

Check your Min Pin regularly for fleas and ticks. If you do find any parasites, use a spray or powder to eradicate them. Remember also to treat your dog's bedding, and spray the parts of the house where he or she has access too. As you will not allow your dog to roam the streets, it is unlikely that you will find parasites a serious problem.

A healthy Min Pin should not be bathed too often. This is because bathing is inclined to remove the natural oils which keep the skin soft, and prevents it from drying and cracking which can result in eczema.

A concrete yard or play area is ideal for Min Pins to run about on as it helps to keep their toe nails short, thus reducing the need to clip them quite often. If the dog is constantly running about on soft ground, or in the house on carpets, then the nails will grow long, and if left unchecked it will force the dog's feet to spread, and in extreme cases this could cause lameness. A special tool can be purchased for this purpose, most good pet shops should stock what you require. If you are not comfortable with clipping the toe nails yourself, a vet would do the job for you. You can however file the nails every few weeks using an ordinary nail file. I know of one owner who actually does this, and although it takes her some considerable time, to get the claws down to a satisfactory length, the dog is quite content to sit and have his manicure. Care should be taken when clipping the nails because some dogs have black nails, and it is therefore difficult to see the quick which if cut into could cause bleeding.

nail clippers

If your dog has foul smelling breath, other than the usual doggy smell which most have, then it is a sign that something is wrong, and a visit to the vet is advisable. Do keep a check on your dog's teeth, and if necessary clean them . It is possible to purchase both toothpaste and brush, especially designed for your dog's needs from your local vet or pet store.

There is a chicken flavoured toothpaste on the market, and it is sure to be a big hit with your canine friend. Do not neglect this area of your dog's health as Periodontal (gum) disease is the cause of many other ailments. Plaque can build up on your dog's teeth. This in turn harbours bacteria which can cause serious health problems, especially if the bacteria enters the bloodstream via the gum tissue and roots of the teeth.

It is quite safe to give your Min Pin garlic tablets, and these can be bought from any pet store. The use of garlic helps prevent many health problems. One a day is sufficient, whether your Min Pin is six months old or six years.

There are also many herbal remedies on the market, and choosing the right product for your Min Pin, can in some circumstances turn out to be the answer to many a problem. I know of one lady who was being driven mad by her Min Pin's behaviour. She had a pair of Min Pins from which she had bred successfully. However, the bitch took a sudden dislike to the dog, and would not have him near her at any price. Their owner was at her wits end, not knowing how to cure the situation. Then she heard about herbal treatment. The bitch was given small doses of Camomile tea, which she loved. Within days she had settled down to being her old loveable self, and peace was once more restored in the home.

Properly cared for, your Min Pin will give you years of pleasure as they live well into their teens, and their loyal and loveable nature will guarantee them a special place in your heart. They are the little toy with a whole lot of dog inside. Play is essential to their well being, and they are ready to play at all times.

One area you might not have considered for your dog is insurance. Vets fees can be very expensive, and no matter how careful you are in caring for your animals welfare, accidents and illness do happen.

There are a number of insurers to choose from, and picking the right policy needs a lot of careful planning. Do not settle for the first premium you come across, shop around, and if necessary ask your vet for advice. Many of them have their own preferences, Petplan being a popular choice as they also allow you to pay by monthly installments.

Protecting your Min Pin in this way ensures peace of mind. Everyone hopes the worst will not happen, but if it did, your dog would be able to receive the best medical attention without you having to worry about a costly bill.

Black and Tan Miniature Pinschers are prone to button tumours, more so than the other colours of the species. While these tumours are more often than not benign, an operation is needed to remove them.

There is also a condition called slipping patella which affects many dogs. It is caused by the knee, slipping out of place. If you perceive your dog holding his paw aloft, he may well be suffering from this complaint. A simple operation will soon have him back on his feet. With all the various illnesses and diseases your dog can fall victim to, having insurance makes sense.

A well groomed family. Proud father stands guard, While Mum keeps watch on her off spring.

6

BREEDING

If you have a bitch and wish to breed from her, it is better if she does not mate the first or second time that she comes into season. A sign that your bitch is on heat, will be a swelling of the vulva, and a show of blood, which later changes to a clear discharge. It is around the 11th to 14th day when the bitch is most receptive to a male. A miniature Pinscher bitch usually comes into season at around six to nine months of age, and then every five or six months although this can vary from one Min Pin to another.

Do not look upon breeding from your bitch as a way of making money. This is totally the wrong attitude to take, and many a breeder will tell you that excessive breeding can lead to a breakdown in the animals health. The Kennel Club will only allow you to register a litter from the same female no more than six times, and rightly so. Also they will not accept registration for puppies born to a bitch over eight years of age unless there are special circumstances to take into consideration.

If you own a pair of Miniature Pinschers, provided they are in no way related, and you wish to breed from them, then it is quite feasible to do so. Always take the bitch to the dog. If the dog shows little or no interest, then you must wait and try again. When mating does take place, the pair will be joined together for anything up to twenty minutes, and will be positioned back to back. If you do not have a dog, but still wish to breed from your bitch, then a stud dog can be provided. However, you may experience some difficulty here. As there are a number of unscrupulous breeders around, do not take it too badly if your request for a stud dog is turned down. The Miniature Pinscher Club, and others, have only the dog's best interests at heart. There is too much inbreeding, carried out by those only interested in making a quick buck. Such inbreeding causes suffering and heartache for these animals as the following story shows only too well............................

`I don't remember much from the place where I was born. It was cramped and dark, and we were never played with by the Humans. I remember my Mum, and her soft fur, but she was often sick, and very thin. She had hardly any milk for me and my brothers and sisters. I remember many of them dying, and I missed them so. I do remember the day I was taken from Mum. I was so sad and scared. My milk teeth had only just come through, and I should have been with Mum Still, but she was so sick, and the Humans kept saying that they wanted money, and were sick of the `mess` that me and my sister made. So we were crated up and taken to a strange place. Just the two of us. We huddled together, and were scared. Still no Human hands came to pet or love us.

So many sights and sounds, and smells. We are in a store where there are many different animals! Some squawk!, some meow! My sister and I are jammed into a small cage. I hear other puppies here. I see Humans look at me. I like the `Little Humans`, they look so sweet and full of fun, like they wanted to play with me.

All day we stay in the small cage. Sometimes, mean people will hit the glass, and frighten us. Every once in a while, we are taken out, to be held or shown to Humans. Some are gentle, others hurt us. They say, `How cute, I want one`, but we never get to go with them.

My sister died last night, when the store was dark. I lay my head on her soft fur, and felt the life leave her small thin body. I heard she was sick, and that I should be sold at a discount price, so that I would quickly leave the store. My soft whine, was the only way I could show, I mourned for her as she was taken out of the cage in the morning, and dumped.

Today, a family came and bought me! Oh happy day! They are a nice family. They really wanted me! They bought a dish and some food, and the little girl held me so tenderly in her arms. I love her so much. The Mum and Dad say what a sweet and good puppy I am. They call me Angel. The family take such good care of me. They gently teach me right from wrong, give me food, and lots of love. I want only to please these wonderful people. I love the little girl, and I enjoy running, and playing with her.

Today I went to the veterinarian. It was a strange place, and I was frightened. I had some injections. My best friend, the little girl held me softly. She said it would be OK, so I relaxed. The vet must have said sad words to my beloved family because they looked unhappy.

Words like.....Severe hip dysplacia, and something about my heart. The vet mentioned something about, `Back Yard breeders, and my parents not being tested. I know not what it means, but it hurts me to see my family so sad. They still love me, and I love them.

I am 6 months old now. Where most other puppies are robust and rowdy, it hurts me just to move. It hurts to run, and play with the little girl, and I find it hard to breathe. I keep trying to be the strong pup I know I should be, but it is so hard.

The little girl is so sad, and Mum and Dad too. I have been to the vets several times now, and the news is never good. He talks about, `Congenital Problems`. I just want to feel the warm sunshine, and run and play, and nuzzle up to my family.

Last night was worse. The pain does not leave me now. It even hurts me to get up for a drink. I am taken in the car one last time. Everyone is so sad, and I don't know why. Have I been bad? I try to be good and loving. What have I done wrong? Oh! if only this pain would go away. If only I could soothe the little girl's tears. I reach over, to lick her hand, but can only whine in pain.

The veterinarian's table is so cold, and I am frightened. The family all hug and love me. They cry into my soft fur. I can feel their love and sadness. I want to lick their soft hands. Even the vet doesn't seem so scary. Today he is gentle, and I sense some kind of relief for my pain. The little girl holds me, and I thank her for giving me so much love. I feel a soft pinch in my foreleg. The pain is beginning to subside. A feeling of peace is overwhelming me. My vision is dreamlike, and I can see my mother, and my brothers and sisters, in a far off green place. They tell me there is no pain there, only peace and happiness. I tell the family good bye. I had hoped to spend many happy years with them, but it was not meant to be.

`You see,` I hear the vet say `Pet shop puppies do not come from ethical breeders`. The pain ends now. I know it will be many years before I see my beloved family again. If only things could have been different.`

Copyright 1999 J. Ellis..

This bitch gave birth to a solitary pup, which weighed just 4 ounces.

Here is the 4 ounce puppy, now an adult.

Still wishing to breed from your Min Pin bitch, you have found a stud dog, taken the bitch to him, and she is now pregnant. It has been known for Miniature Pinschers to have phantom pregnancies, but we will assume this is not so at this time.

The gestation period should be counted 9 weeks from the day of mating, but this is not always the case. You must treat the pregnant Min Pin with the care and attention she deserves. To begin with, her diet can remain the same, but as she progresses into her pregnancy, it is advisable to increase the amount of food given. You may also include a vitamin supplement.SA 37 tablets, available from most pet stores are suitable for complimentary feeding. While some breeders recommend a supplement, others are against it. It is purely a matter of personal preference.

When the time comes for her to give birth, make certain you will be around. She should by now, be in a whelping box, and if other animals are around, it would be wise to contain her in a large cage, out of harms way. Very few Min Pins give birth easily. It may be necessary for you to assist in the delivery. Have the vets phone number handy, in case you need to consult him for advice.. Should the first pup be still born (it does happen), on no account should you remove it from the mother until another has taken its place. To do so could cause the bitch stress, and might prevent her from delivering her other pup or puppies safely.

It is normal for Min Pins to have three or four puppies, but there are exceptions to the rule. A new born Min Pin will weigh about 4 ounces, and quite easily fit into the palm of ones hand.

If you own more than two bitches between the ages of 8 months -8 years, provided they have not been spayed, then you must have a breeders licence.

A pregnant bitch waits patiently for the arrival of her puppies.

Whelping Chart

TABLE SHOWING WHEN A BITCH IS DUE TO WHELP

Served January	Due to Whelp March	Served February	Due to Whelp April	Served March	Due to Whelp May	Served April	Due to Whelp June	Served May	Due to Whelp July	Served June	Due to Whelp August	Served July	Due to Whelp September	Served August	Due to Whelp October	Served September	Due to Whelp November	Served October	Due to Whelp December	Served November	Due to Whelp January	Served December	Due to Whelp February
1	5	1	5	1	3	1	3	1	3	1	3	1	2	1	3	1	3	1	3	1	3	1	2
2	6	2	6	2	4	2	4	2	4	2	4	2	3	2	4	2	4	2	4	2	4	2	3
3	7	3	7	3	5	3	5	3	5	3	5	3	5	3	5	3	5	3	5	3	5	3	4
4	8	4	8	4	6	4	6	4	6	4	6	4	6	4	6	4	6	4	6	4	6	4	5
5	9	5	9	5	7	5	7	5	7	5	7	5	6	5	7	5	7	5	7	5	7	5	6
6	10	6	10	6	8	6	8	6	8	6	8	6	7	6	8	6	8	6	8	6	8	6	7
7	11	7	11	7	9	7	9	7	9	7	9	7	8	7	9	7	9	7	9	7	9	7	8
8	12	8	12	8	10	8	10	8	10	8	10	8	9	8	10	8	10	8	10	8	10	8	9
9	13	9	13	9	11	9	11	9	11	9	11	9	10	9	11	9	11	9	11	9	11	9	10
10	14	10	14	10	12	10	12	10	12	10	12	10	11	10	12	10	12	10	12	10	12	10	11
11	15	11	15	11	13	11	13	11	13	11	13	11	12	11	13	11	13	11	13	11	13	11	12
12	16	12	16	12	14	12	14	12	14	12	14	12	13	12	14	12	14	12	14	12	14	12	13
13	17	13	17	13	15	13	15	13	15	13	15	13	14	13	15	13	15	13	15	13	15	13	14
14	18	14	18	14	16	14	16	14	16	14	16	14	15	14	16	14	16	14	16	14	16	14	15
15	19	15	19	15	17	15	17	15	17	15	17	15	16	15	17	15	17	15	17	15	17	15	16
16	20	16	20	16	18	16	18	16	18	16	18	16	17	16	18	16	18	16	18	16	18	16	17
17	21	17	21	17	19	17	19	17	19	17	19	17	18	17	19	17	19	17	19	17	19	17	18
18	22	18	22	18	20	18	20	18	20	18	20	18	19	18	20	18	20	18	20	18	20	18	19
19	23	19	23	19	21	19	21	19	21	19	21	19	20	19	21	19	21	19	21	19	21	19	20
20	24	20	24	20	22	20	22	20	22	20	22	20	21	20	22	20	22	20	22	20	22	20	21
21	25	21	25	21	23	21	23	21	23	21	23	21	22	21	23	21	23	21	23	21	23	21	22
22	26	22	26	22	24	22	24	22	24	22	24	22	23	22	24	22	24	22	24	22	24	22	23
23	27	23	27	23	25	23	25	23	25	23	25	23	24	23	25	23	25	23	25	23	25	23	24
24	28	24	28	24	26	24	26	24	26	24	26	24	25	24	26	24	26	24	26	24	26	24	25
25	29	25	29	25	27	25	27	25	27	25	27	25	26	25	27	25	27	25	27	25	27	25	26
26	30	26	30	26	28	26	28	26	28	26	28	26	27	26	28	26	28	26	28	26	28	26	27
					MAY																		
27	31	27	1	27	29	27	29	27	29	27	29	27	28	27	29	27	29	27	29	27	29	27	28
	APR.																						MAR.
28	1	28	2	28	30	28	30	28	30	28	30	28	29	28	30	28	30	28	30	28	30	28	1
					JULY																		
29	2	29		3	29	31	29	1	29	31	29	30	29	31	29	31	29	31	29	31	29	2
					JUNE			AUG.		SEP.		OCT.		NOV.		DEC.		JAN.		FEB.			
30	3			30	1	30	2	30	1	30	1	30	1	30	1	30	2	30	1	30	3		
31	4			31	2			31	2			31	2	31	2			31	2			31	4

An especially designed cage for Mum and her puppies

Viewed from above, the cage is ideal for protecting the bitch and her puppies.

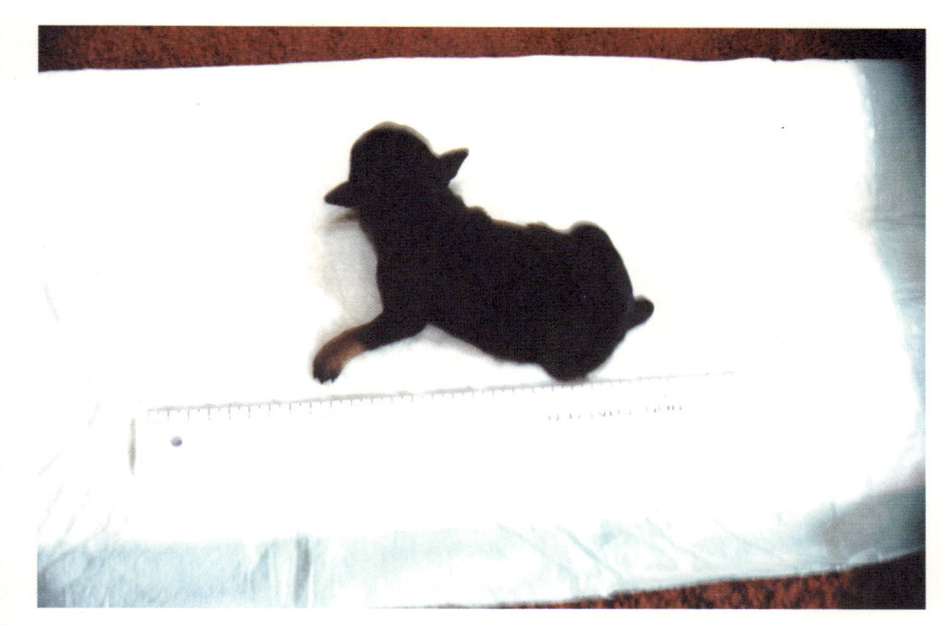

A Black and Tan Male puppy, 8 days old.

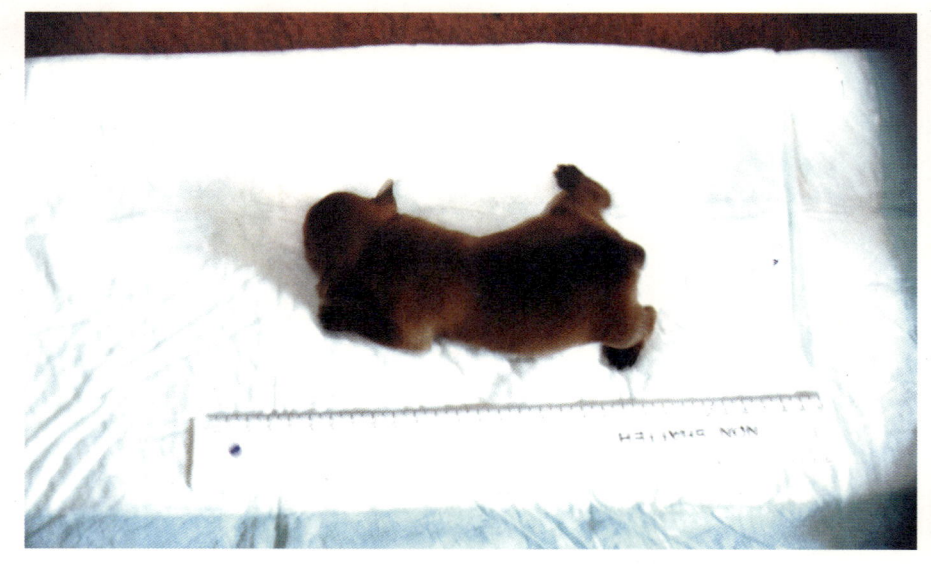

A Red bitch, 8 days old.

Miniature Pinscher Illustrated Breed Standard

General Appearance:

Well Balanced, sturdy, compact, elegant, short coupled, smooth-coated, toy dog. Naturally well groomed, proud, vigorous and alert.

Characteristics:

Precise hackney gait, fearless animation, complete self possession and spirited presence.

Temperament:

Fearless and alert.

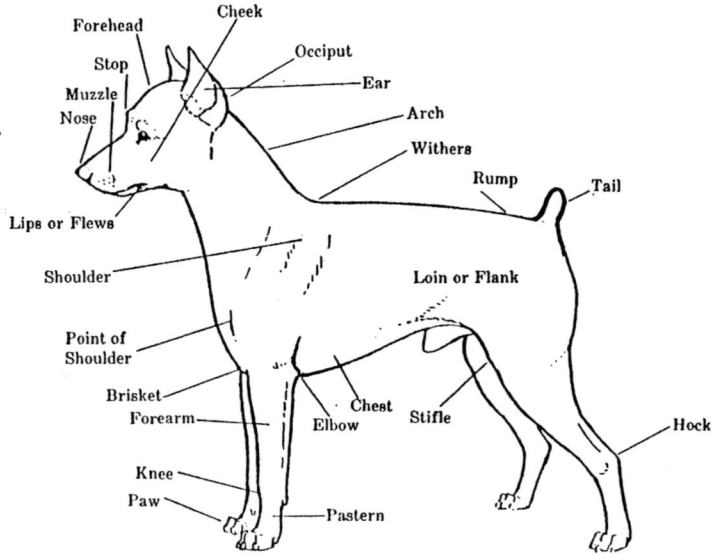

Head and Skull:

More elongated than short and round. Narrow, without conspicuous cheek formation. In proportion to body. Skull flat when viewed from front. Muzzle rather strong and proportionate to skull. Nostrils well formed. Nose black with the exception of chocolate and blue, in which it may be self-coloured.

1) Correctly balanced head
2) Lacking under jaw.
3) Lacking under jaw, no stop and incorrect swan neck.

Eyes:

Fitting well into face. Neither too full nor round, nor too small or slanting. Black or nearly black.

Ears:

Set on high, as small as possible, erect or dropped.

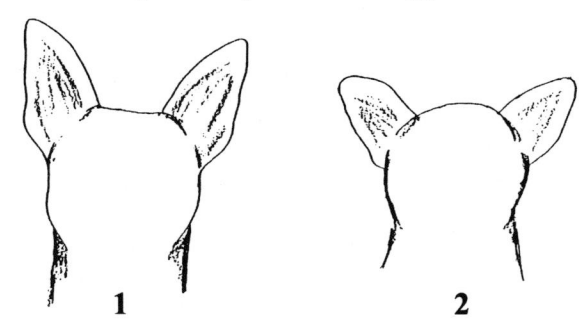

1) Correct high set ears with flat skull.

2) Incorrect low set ears with rounded skull.

Mouth:

Jaws strong, with a perfect, regular and complete scissor bite, i.e. the upper teeth closely overlapping the lower teeth and set squarer to the jaws.

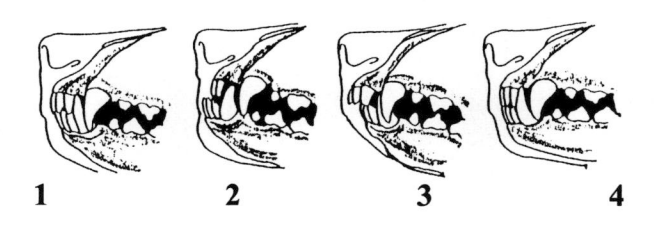

1) Correct scissor bite.   **2)** Incorrect undershot.   **3)** Incorrect overshot.
4) Incorrect level bite.

Neck:

Strong yet graceful, slightly arched. Well fitted into shoulders. free from throatiness.

Forequarters:

Forechest well developed and full, moderately broad, shoulders clean, sloping with moderate angulation. Legs straight, medium bone, elbows close to body.

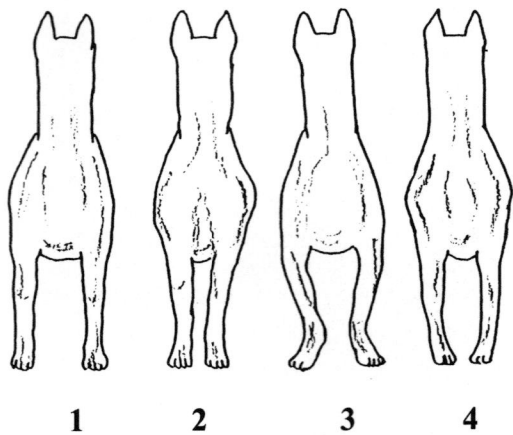

1) Moderately broad chest, correct straight front.

2) Narrow chest and out at elbow.

3) Fiddle front, the feet are turned outwards.

4) Loose elbows, the elbows are turned outwards and the feet inwards.

Body:

square, back line straight, sloping towards rear. Belly moderately tucked up. Ribs well sprung, deep rather than barrelled. Viewed from top slightly wedge shaped.

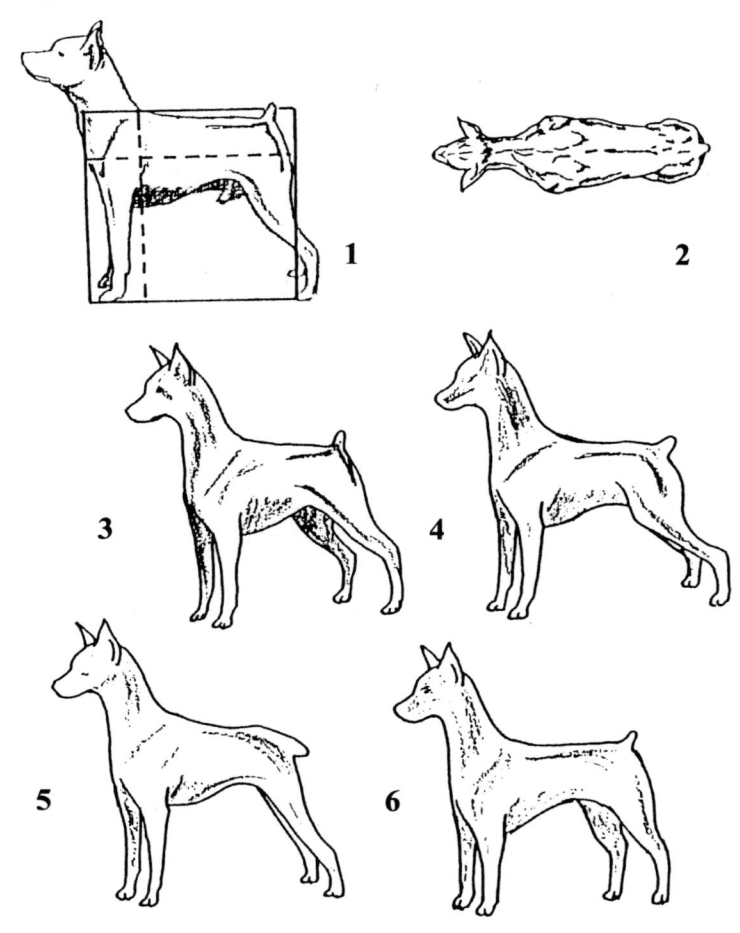

1) Square Min Pin; 2) View from above; 3) A correctly balanced Min Pin;
4) Over angulated; 5) Too straight in stifle; 6) body too long, short in leg.

Hindquarters:

Parallel and wide enough apart to fit in with a properly built body. Hindquarters well developed, muscular with good sweep of stifle, and hocks turning neither in nor out. Legs straight, medium bone.

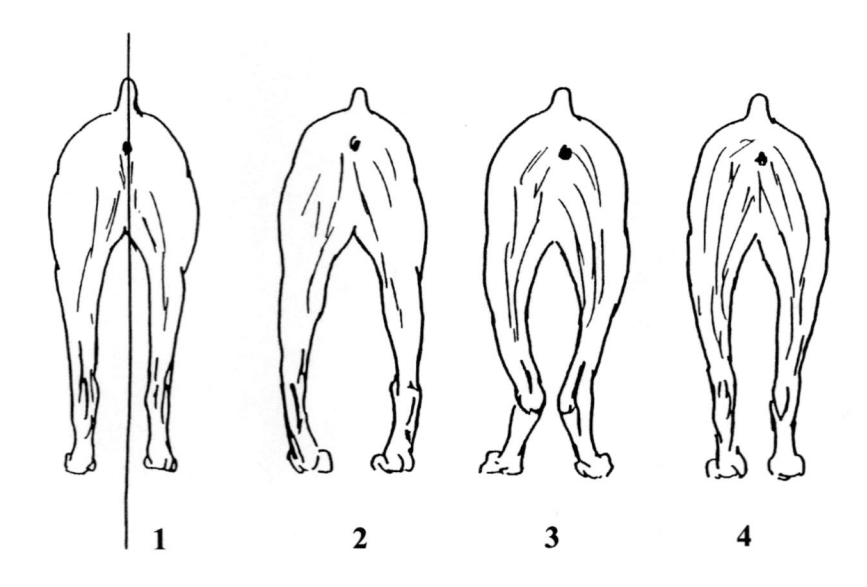

1) Correct.

2) Barrel Hocked, feet turning in.

3) Cow Hocked, feet turning out.

4) Narrow, a fault which becomes obvious on the move.

Tail:

Continuation of topline carried a little high and customarily docked short.

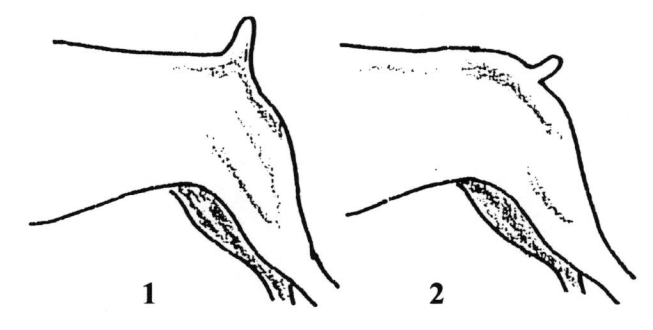

1) Correct high set tail; **2)** Dropped croup, low set tail.

Feet:

Cat-like; nails dark.

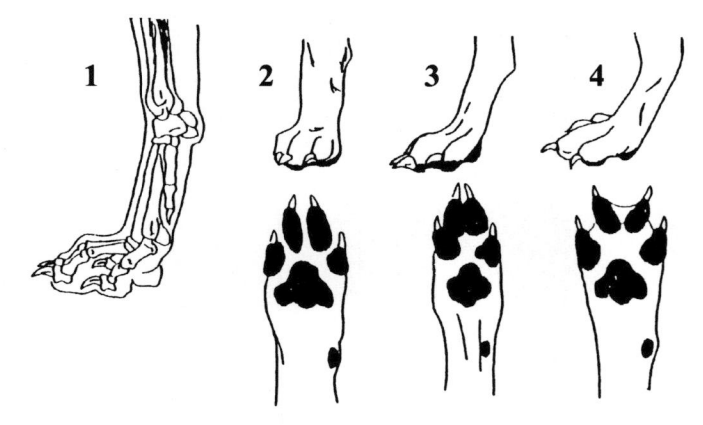

1) Skeleton drawing of the correct foot;

2) Cat foot, round and compact;

3) Hare foot, an elongated oval foot;

4) Splay foot, this is a fault.

Gait/Movement:

Co-ordinated to permit a true hackneyed action.

1) Correct

2) No rear drive.

3) Goose-step, good rear drive;

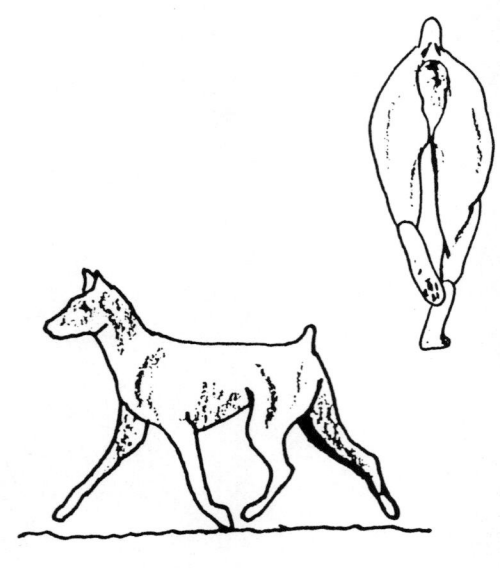

4) Straight front, crossing rear.

Colour:

Black, blue, chocolate with sharply defined tan markings on cheeks, lips, lower jaw, throat, twin spots above eyes and chest, lower half of forelegs, inside of hindlegs and vent region, lower portion of hocks and feet. All above colours have black pencilling on toes without thumb marks. Solid red of various shades. Slight white on chest permissible but undesirable.

Size:

Height from 25.5-30cm(10-12ins) at withers.

Faults:

Any departure from the foregoing points is to be considered a fault and the seriousness with which the fault is regarded should be in exact proportion to its degree.

Note:

Male animals should have two apparently normal testicles fully descended into the scrotum.

Standard Regarding Coat:

Coat- Smooth, hard and short, straight and lustrous, closely adhering to and uniformly covering the body.

Faults-

Thin, too long, dull, upstanding, curly dry, areas of various thickness or bald spots.

Breed Note:

The Miniature Pinscher is a German development of the toy terrier and has been known in Germany and other European countries for centuries. There are old illustrations showing the breed as a ratter and he still retains his keenness as a watch dog. He seems unaware of his own small size in protecting home and family.

The breed has done well in the show ring where judges appreciate his stylish, high stepping action and his alert demeanour. He makes an admirable, clean pet for any size home and is suitable to the family with older children.

Grooming Procedure:

A Miniature Pinscher's grooming requirements are negligible and for the house pet, brushing several times a week will keep the coat and skin in good condition.

For the show ring it is also advisable to trim the coarse feelers from the muzzle, above the eyes and face moles. Any long hair such as is found on the sides of the neck, and up the backs of front and hind legs should be trimmed or thinned as needed to give the desired, sleek appearance.

Particular attention should be paid to the feet and in this connection the nails should be shortened regularly to achieve, a tight compact foot. Nothing looks worse than a Miniature Pinscher whose nails have been neglected. Such a dog will show thin feet with ugly, outspread toes, an avoidable blemish.

8

THE LOYAL FRIEND

Miniature Pinschers make excellent guard dogs, as my daughter Susan found out recently. Sue has three Min Pins, Tas, Tika and Pepsi.

Last Summer workmen called at her home to install doubleglazing. Tas, a black and Tan male barked so ferociously that one of the workmen refused to enter. Not until the little creature was safely shut up in the kitchen would he cross the threshold. Actually the workman didn't know it at the time, but it was a case of the Min Pin's bark being worse than his bite.

However there was another occasion when quite the opposite was true. It was late Summer, and Sue was in the kitchen ironing. At that time Sue only had two Min Pins, Tas, and Tika a red coloured bitch.

Both dogs were restless, and began barking to go outside. Thinking they wanted to relieve themselves Sue opened the back door and let them out. The next instance such a commotion was heard coming from outside coupled with agonising screams.
Sue lay down her iron, and ran out to investigate. What she saw was beyond belief. An angry Tas was hanging by the teeth from a strangers buttocks. The intruder had been in the garden when the dogs had been let

out. He had discreetly ducked down behind a low fence, but Tas had sniffed him out, and before the man could stand up, the courageous little dog had sunk his teeth into the man's posterior. Tika was running round and round the intruder barking for all she was worth.

The man, a youth in his late twenties was standing up with Tas swaying in the air from his behind, the little dog's teeth well and truly locked on to his prey. No matter how the man hit out at Tas trying to knock him off, the brave little dog held fast.

Susan's first reaction was one of anger. Here was an intruder in her garden with no authority to be there, and he was behaving violently towards her precious Min Pin. When she had grasped the situation, she told the man to stand still. Tika was picked up and taken indoors.

It took the handle of a yard broom to prise Tas`s teeth from the man's backside, which by now had blood seeping through his jeans. When questioned the man said he had come into the garden to retrieve a ball. `A likely story", Sue replied, knowing there had been a number of break ins in the area she was likely suspicious. The man did not hang around. He made quick his escape by climbing the high fence which surrounded the garden, the same way he had obviously entered. His wound would have required treatment, and possibly a visit to the

Miniature Pinscher Illustrated Breed Standard

General Appearance:

Well Balanced, sturdy, compact, elegant, short coupled, smooth-coated, toy dog. Naturally well groomed, proud, vigorous and alert.

Characteristics:

Precise hackney gait, fearless animation, complete self possession and spirited presence.

Temperament:

Fearless and alert.

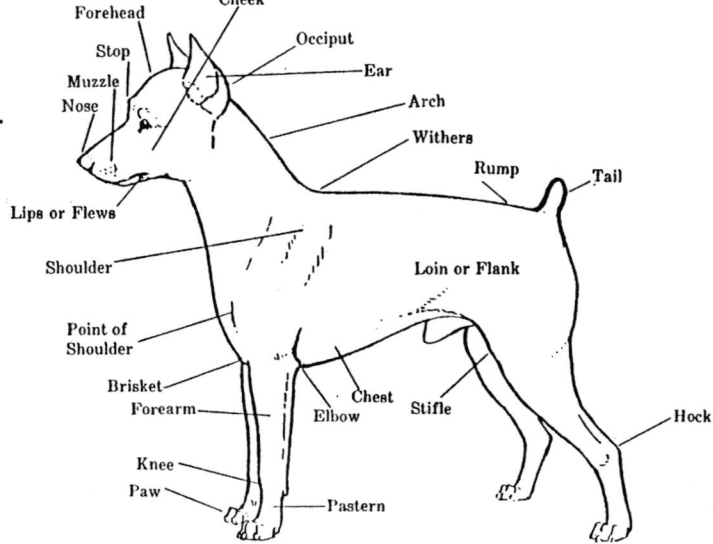

Head and Skull:

More elongated than short and round. Narrow, without conspicuous cheek formation. In proportion to body. Skull flat when viewed from front. Muzzle rather strong and proportionate to skull. Nostrils well formed. Nose black with the exception of chocolate and blue, in which it may be self-coloured.

1) Correctly balanced head
2) Lacking under jaw.
3) Lacking under jaw, no stop and incorrect swan neck.

Eyes:

Fitting well into face. Neither too full nor round, nor too small or slanting. Black or nearly black.

Ears:

Set on high, as small as possible, erect or dropped.

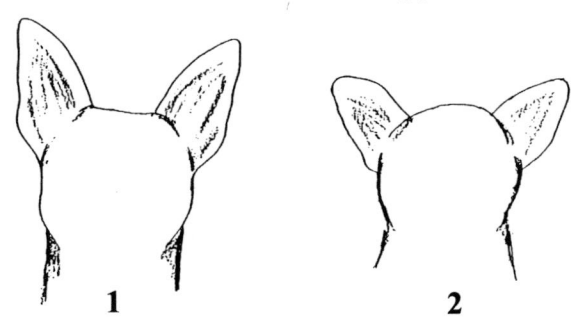

1) Correct high set ears with flat skull.

2) Incorrect low set ears with rounded skull.

Mouth:

Jaws strong, with a perfect, regular and complete scissor bite, i.e. the upper teeth closely overlapping the lower teeth and set squarer to the jaws.

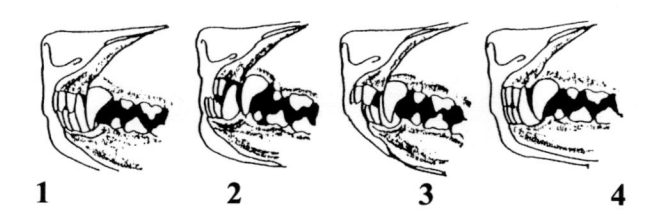

1) Correct scissor bite.   **2)** Incorrect undershot.   **3)** Incorrect overshot.
4) Incorrect level bite.

Neck:

Strong yet graceful, slightly arched. Well fitted into shoulders. free from throatiness.

Forequarters:

Forechest well developed and full, moderately broad, shoulders clean, sloping with moderate angulation. Legs straight, medium bone, elbows close to body.

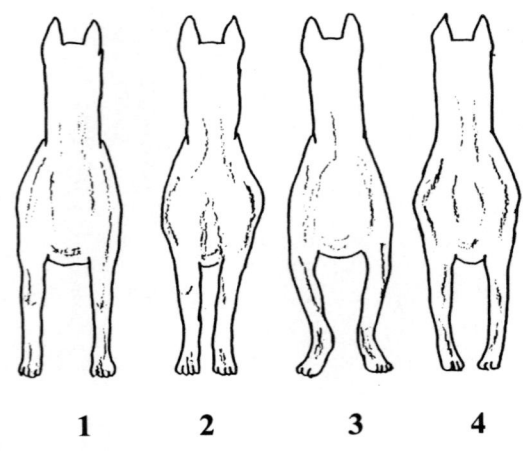

1) Moderately broad chest, correct straight front.

2) Narrow chest and out at elbow.

3) Fiddle front, the feet are turned outwards.

4) Loose elbows, the elbows are turned outwards and the feet inwards.

Body:

square, back line straight, sloping towards rear. Belly moderately tucked up. Ribs well sprung, deep rather than barrelled. Viewed from top slightly wedge shaped.

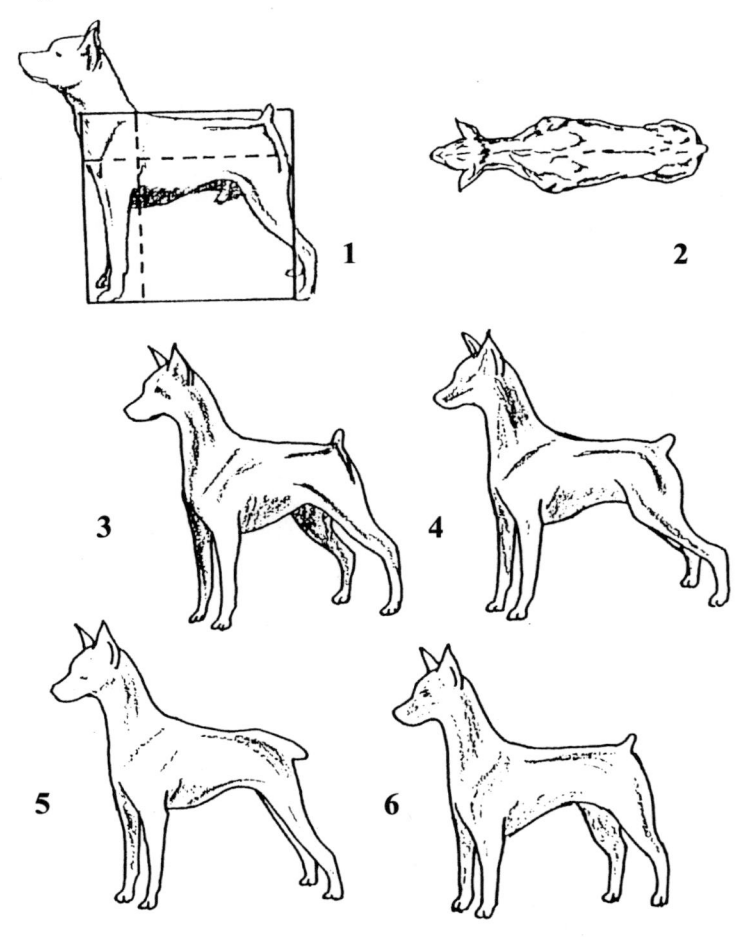

1) Square Min Pin; 2) View from above; 3) A correctly balanced Min Pin; 4) Over angulated; 5) Too straight in stifle; 6) body too long, short in leg.

Hindquarters:

Parallel and wide enough apart to fit in with a properly built body. Hindquarters well developed, muscular with good sweep of stifle, and hocks turning neither in nor out. Legs straight, medium bone.

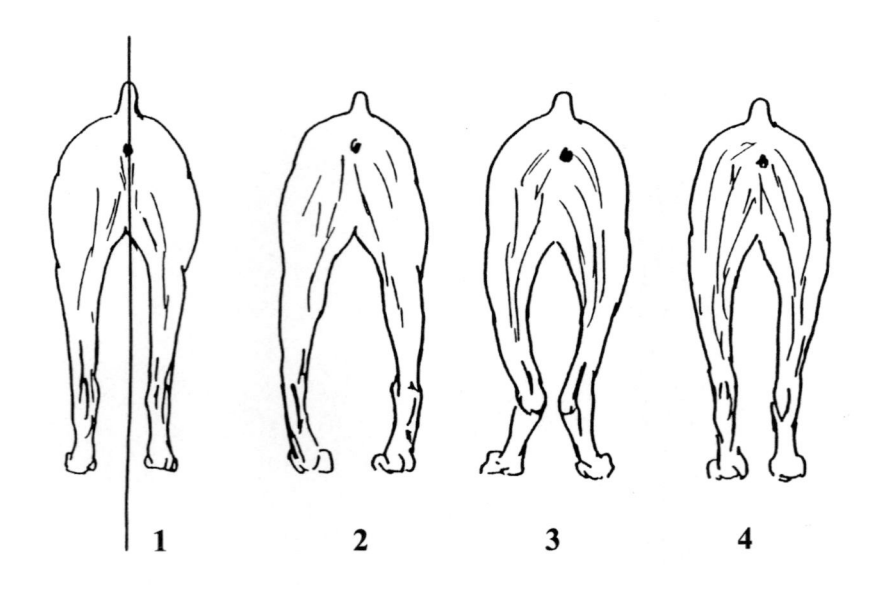

1) Correct.

2) Barrel Hocked, feet turning in.

3) Cow Hocked, feet turning out.

4) Narrow, a fault which becomes obvious on the move.

Tail:

Continuation of topline carried a little high and customarily docked short.

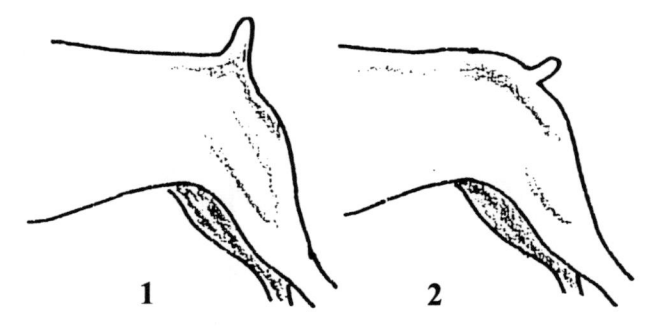

1) Correct high set tail; **2)** Dropped croup, low set tail.

Feet:

Cat-like; nails dark.

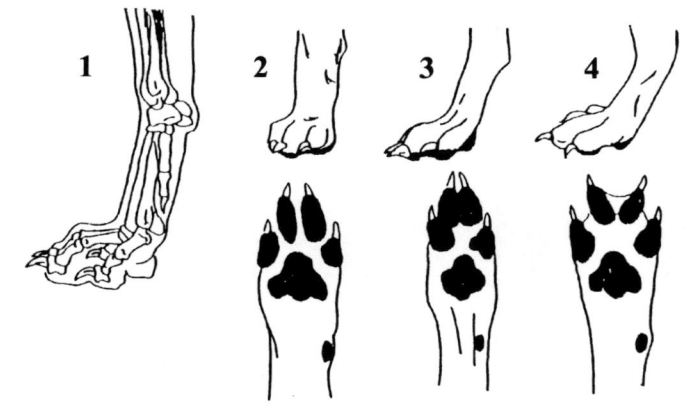

1) Skeleton drawing of the correct foot;

2) Cat foot, round and compact;

3) Hare foot, an elongated oval foot;

4) Splay foot, this is a fault.

Gait/Movement:

Co-ordinated to permit a true hackneyed action.

1) Correct

2) No rear drive.

3) Goose-step, good rear drive;

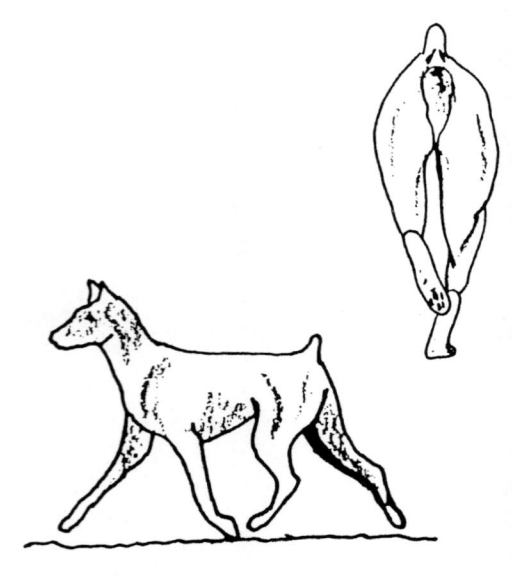

4) Straight front, crossing rear.

Colour:

Black, blue, chocolate with sharply defined tan markings on cheeks, lips, lower jaw, throat, twin spots above eyes and chest, lower half of forelegs, inside of hindlegs and vent region, lower portion of hocks and feet. All above colours have black pencilling on toes without thumb marks. Solid red of various shades. Slight white on chest permissible but undesirable.

Size:

Height from 25.5-30cm(10-12ins) at withers.

Faults:

Any departure from the foregoing points is to be considered a fault and the seriousness with which the fault is regarded should be in exact proportion to its degree.

Note:

Male animals should have two apparently normal testicles fully descended into the scrotum.

Standard Regarding Coat:

Coat- Smooth, hard and short, straight and lustrous, closely adhering to and uniformly covering the body.

Faults-

Thin, too long, dull, upstanding, curly dry, areas of various thickness or bald spots.

Breed Note:

The Miniature Pinscher is a German development of the toy terrier and has been known in Germany and other European countries for centuries. There are old illustrations showing the breed as a ratter and he still retains his keenness as a watch dog. He seems unaware of his own small size in protecting home and family.
The breed has done well in the show ring where judges appreciate his stylish, high stepping action and his alert demeanour. He makes an admirable, clean pet for any size home and is suitable to the family with older children.

Grooming Procedure:

A Miniature Pinscher's grooming requirements are negligible and for the house pet, brushing several times a week will keep the coat and skin in good condition.

For the show ring it is also advisable to trim the coarse feelers from the muzzle, above the eyes and face moles. Any long hair such as is found on the sides of the neck, and up the backs of front and hind legs should be trimmed or thinned as needed to give the desired, sleek appearance.

Particular attention should be paid to the feet and in this connection the nails should be shortened regularly to achieve, a tight compact foot. Nothing looks worse than a Miniature Pinscher whose nails have been neglected. Such a dog will show thin feet with ugly, outspread toes, an avoidable blemish.

8

THE LOYAL FRIEND

Miniature Pinschers make excellent guard dogs, as my daughter Susan found out recently. Sue has three Min Pins, Tas, Tika and Pepsi.

Last Summer workmen called at her home to install doubleglazing. Tas, a black and Tan male barked so ferociously that one of the workmen refused to enter. Not until the little creature was safely shut up in the kitchen would he cross the threshold. Actually the workman didn't know it at the time, but it was a case of the Min Pin's bark being worse than his bite.

However there was another occasion when quite the opposite was true. It was late Summer, and Sue was in the kitchen ironing. At that time Sue only had two Min Pins, Tas, and Tika a red coloured bitch.

Both dogs were restless, and began barking to go outside. Thinking they wanted to relieve themselves Sue opened the back door and let them out. The next instance such a commotion was heard coming from outside coupled with agonising screams.
Sue lay down her iron, and ran out to investigate. What she saw was beyond belief. An angry Tas was hanging by the teeth from a strangers buttocks. The intruder had been in the garden when the dogs had been let

out. He had discreetly ducked down behind a low fence, but Tas had sniffed him out, and before the man could stand up, the courageous little dog had sunk his teeth into the man's posterior. Tika was running round and round the intruder barking for all she was worth.

The man, a youth in his late twenties was standing up with Tas swaying in the air from his behind, the little dog's teeth well and truly locked on to his prey. No matter how the man hit out at Tas trying to knock him off, the brave little dog held fast.

Susan's first reaction was one of anger. Here was an intruder in her garden with no authority to be there, and he was behaving violently towards her precious Min Pin. When she had grasped the situation, she told the man to stand still. Tika was picked up and taken indoors.

It took the handle of a yard broom to prise Tas`s teeth from the man's backside, which by now had blood seeping through his jeans. When questioned the man said he had come into the garden to retrieve a ball. `A likely story", Sue replied, knowing there had been a number of break ins in the area she was likely suspicious. The man did not hang around. He made quick his escape by climbing the high fence which surrounded the garden, the same way he had obviously entered. His wound would have required treatment, and possibly a visit to the doctor for a Tetanus jab. How I would love to have been a fly on the wall in the surgery when the man explained how he came by his injury.

***

The tale of Pepsi Min Pin is one which defies belief. Sue had seen an advert in a trade paper, advertising an eighteen month old Black and Tan female Miniature Pinscher for sale. For sometime Sue had been contemplating buying another dog, and she jumped at the chance of owning this one. The owner lived in Manchester. A telephone call confirmed the dog was still for sale, so over to Manchester Sue went.

Pepsi was in the kitchen with the back door wide open. Beyond stood a wooden frame covered with wire mesh. In the frame stood two other pedigree dogs, not Min Pins but possibly Spaniels. Sue was told that Pepsi shared the frame with the two dogs. It was obvious Pepsi had been neglected. She was skin and bone without any covering of fur on the back of her ears. To have walked away from the poor creature would have been like handing her a death sentence. She would not have survived beyond two weeks. Out of love and compassion for the tiny scrap, Sue bought her, and took her home. The first thing she did was to give Pepsi a much needed bath.

She weighed just four and a half pounds. Her nails had grown so

An emaciated Pepsi, before she was nursed back to health.

long her feet were beginning to splay, and she had an eye infection which required immediate attention. A visit to the vet the next day helped her on the way to recovery. She was given Betamethasone drops for her eyes, a booster injection, worming tablets and had her nails cut. The veterinary treatment is ongoing, and with love and care, Pepsi now weighs five pounds three ounces, but it is a long hard struggle getting her completely well. Even the vet did not believe Pepsi was eighteen months old until he looked in her mouth. The size of her teeth confirmed it.

Susan found out that she was Pepsi's fourth owner since birth including the breeder, who when contacted was most distressed to say the least. Pepsi was still registered with the breeder because not one of her previous owners had bothered to register change of ownership. Her previous owner was reported to the necessary authorities.

The case of Pepsi Min Pin brings to mind the wonderful work carried out by Susan Colborne-Baber. She runs the Miniature Pinscher rescue. Susan has owned and bred Miniature Pinschers for fourteen years. Her work started in 1986 when she was asked to help find a home for a little Miniature Pinscher bitch called Beauty. Since then Susan, and her veterinary friend Di Stark, has helped many Miniature Pinschers to find new and loving homes. It is to these good women, and others like them that the following poem has been dedicated.

DEDICATED TO PEOPLE IN RESCUE

I wasn't a pup when I came to your home,
I'd been dumped on the road, left to roam.
Don't remember the people except the pain,
They left me to die in the cold and the rain.
You were driving along, it was late at night,
When you saw the faintest glimmer of light.
You took a chance and turned around,
Got out of the van and knelt to the ground.

My quivering body felt the gentlest of hands,
I knew I need not make any demands.
In your heart and your home, there was always room,
For those who would face certain doom.
You healed my body and you healed my heart,
You gave me what I needed, a fresh start.
When I cried at night, you were always there,
With soft words, a kiss, a hug to share,

When I misbehaved and would cower with guilt,
You showed only love....up to the hilt.
You loved and cared for me in sickness and health,

Our love for each other was more precious than wealth.
Even when you were tired and had had a bad day,
You would always come home to me and say,
"I missed you my baby, I am glad to be back",
Then you'd give me a kiss, a hug and a pat.

We'd have a nice dinner, then go out to play,
There was so much love, I wanted to stay.
But my eyes, they faded and my heart grew weak,
As my time grew closer, you could not speak.
You held me tight, tears flowed from your eyes,
We both found it hard to say goodbye.
The release from pain we knew must end,
No more time on this Earth would we spend.

Running in the fields, playing ball,
Sitting quietly together at the end of it all.
But our time together is not through,
Because I will be there waiting for you.
At the edge of the Rainbow Bridge I'll stand,
Until once again I see those gentle hands.
I will run to you with tail held high,
We will never again have to say goodbye.
My love at death, it does not end,
Because you are indeed, a dog's best friend.

Jeane Illsche.

9

PUTTING ON THE STYLE

Did you know, you can now buy furniture for your Miniature Pinscher? While most Min Pins are crated, especially those intended for showing, there are some, who for one reason or another are not.

Perhaps the Min Pin may be ageing, after all, they do live long lives, and having given you the best of their years, shouldn't you now be doing something for them?

`Snaffles` Pet furniture is possibly the best money can buy. I tracked down Charles Morgan, and his Pet furniture, at `CRUFTS`. The `Snaffles stand attracted a lot of interest, not surprising, since the style and workmanship which has gone into the `Snaffles` range of furniture is unique.

The pet beds come in four sizes, each with a specially designed, washable, thermal mattress. The covers can be removed for washing, and come in a choice of three cotton check colours. The beds are

`Snaffles pet beds come in four sizes

sturdy and comfortable, raised off the floor for added protection from drafts. Besides the Pet bed range, `Snaffles` also make a pet chest, ideal for keeping all your Min Pin toys, towels and other odds and ends in.

Pet beds are not the only thing in a dog's life which have become both glamourous, and yet remained practical. Dog coats have also changed over the years. It is now possible to have them made to measure, in a variety of fabrics and designs. I have seen Min Pins wearing army camouflage coats, red satin ones trimmed with fur, and even limitation leopard skins. Dressing up your pet has become big business in some countries, with costumes for weddings, Halloween and other special occasions. Personally, I don't hold with dressing up dogs. The little red bitch on the cover of this book, took a lot of patience, doggy chocolate drops, and many clicks of the camera , before she became bored and ran off.

***

If you have access to the Internet, there are several web pages, devoted to Min Pins. It was while surfing on the net, that my daughter Susan came across `The Min Pin List. Min Pin owners from all over the world, chat regularly, exchanging news and views about their animals. During one conversation, the dialogue went something like this:

'My Min Pin is off his food. Have taken him to the vets, but he can find nothing wrong with him'. Several other Min Pin owners expressed opinions as to what might be the cause of the Min Pin's lack of interest in food.

The following evening, the same owner stated that she had returned to the vet, her dog still being somewhat listless and still not eating. Again, the vet could find nothing wrong. On the third evening, still at her wits end over her Min Pin's behaviour, the lady happened to mention that her dog, while not eating his food, had taken a sudden fancy to a Chinese rug, which she kept in the lounge. She found the animal with a quantity of tufts from the rug, hanging out of its mouth.

This statement set alarm bells ringing in Sue's head. I had a much loved cat called Kitty. Now unknown to me, for I never caught her at it, she was eating the thread from my sewing machine. Kitty began refusing her food, and became very listless. I took her to the vet who could find nothing wrong with her. A blood test indicated an infection so she was given a course of antibiotics. Kitty seemed to rally round, but a week later, she lapsed back into ill health.

Further blood tests followed, all of which proved her to be in perfect health, although by now she was rapidly losing weight. In desperation, I took her to a second vet. She was X-rayed, and found to have an abnormality, which showed up as a lump in her stomach, possibly a tumour. When operated on, the lump turned out to be bunched up sewing thread, which had embedded itself into her intestines and infected them. Sadly, she could not be saved, and was put to sleep while still under the anaesthetic.

Susan, while not wishing to alarm the worried Min Pin's owner, related the story of Kitty to her. The following day, the lady took her Min Pin back to the vet, asking for him to be X-rayed. The X-Ray pin pointed something inside the animal. He was operated on, and a quantity of carpet was removed without any damage to the dog's intestines. Susan received a grateful E- mail from the dog's owner. As Sue pointed out, if it had not been for Kitty, no one would have been any the wiser. Even the vet admitted, an X-ray would have been his last resort, by which time it might well have proved too late. The vet then sent word to other veterinary practices, making them aware of such a situation.

There was some amusement among those who had followed the drama on the Internet, when someone wrote: A dog's life, saved by a cat. How would he ever live it down. Further correspondence from the Min

Pin's owner, stated that the Chinese rug, which had been the cause of all the hassle, had been relegated to the trash bin. Everyone breathed a sigh of relief.

I sincerely hope that any problems you may experience with your Min Pins are few and far between. The pleasure and comfort, these little dog's will bring into your life, far out weighs any unpleasantness.

10

CRUFTS 1999

Of all the dog shows, up and down the country, which take place during the year, none are more spectacular than Crufts. It is without doubt, the world's greatest dog show. To win at Crufts is the ultimate accolade, the aim of every serious Min Pin owner. As yet, a Miniature Pinscher has not taken the title of, `Best in Show`, but the day when this will happen, can surely not be too far away. Already judges are taking more than a passing interest in toy dogs.

Crufts is a four day event, which takes place annually at the National Exhibition Centre in Birmingham. There are five halls, each one the size of an aircraft hanger, this gives you some indication of the vastness of the place. Judging of the various breeds, takes place in all five halls, with different dogs competing on different days.

Besides the show rings, there are a colossal number of stands, all displaying their merchandise, as well as bars and restaurants where one can take the weight off one's feet, sit back, and relax in a pleasant, and friendly atmosphere. The four days at Crufts really are the best dates in the doggy calendar.

The final day of Crufts 1999, fell on March 14th, which also happened to be `Mother's Day`. It was also the day on which Miniature Pinschers were to be judged. The little dogs did not disappoint. They trotted around the ring, head held high, alert and aiming to please.

The judging took place in ring 18 by Mrs Joyce W Mann, who certainly had her work cut out. In Class: 1869- Special Puppy Bitch, the winner was VIVA FOREVER AT HAWKSFLIGHT, `Lulu` a charming red puppy of 10 months, owned by Mackie & Kelland.

The `Best of Breed winner was a Black and Tan, named NEW ERA FOR NETHAN, owned by Mr PETER MCLEAN.

While at Crufts, I ran into Susan Colbourne-Baber and her friend Di Stark, the ladies who rescue ill treated and unwanted Min Pins. They had four Min Pins with them, and had been at Crufts for the whole of the four days, so were really shattered, although the Min Pins they had with them, all looked happy and bright as buttons. One of the Min Pins, Dorothy, had gained second place in the Veteran Bitch. Dorothy was 12 tears old.

Christine Mitchel, Step daughter of Peter Mclean, proudly shows off the `Best of Breed` winner NEW ERA FOR NATHAN. Christine was attending Crufts with her mother.

I asked Di and Susan how many Miniature Pinschers they had of their own, not counting the rescue ones, .They replied nineteen. I gasped!. These ladies are certainly dedicated to the breed. Not only that, they told me they were going to pick up two more rescue Min Pins on their way home.

Di gave me an excellent tip for measuring the height of your Min Pin. Stand the dog against a wall, hold a pencil at the base of the neck, just in front of the Withers, and mark. When the dog moves away, you can then measure the distance from floor to pencil mark.

Sonya Saxby and her husband Alan were also in attendance at Crufts, and it was a pleasure to put a face to the voice I had spoken to on the telephone. They are such a friendly couple.

The whole time I was at Crufts, I only ever heard a dog bark once, which is incredible when you remember how many animals were there.

In the year 2000, the dates for the Crufts show are from 9th-12th March. 2001, 8th-11th March. I look forward to meeting you there. Whether you show or not, Crufts is a venue you should not miss.

RULA ROSTRUM, A delightful red bitch, who is far too fat for the show ring. Her statue is more in keeping with a pot bellied pig. However, she posed beautifully in crown and cloak, proving beyond doubt, that the Miniature Pinscher is indeed, `**THE KING OF TOYS**`.

The Kennel Club
>1-5 Clarges Street,
>Piccadilly,
>London
>W1Y 8AB
>ENGLAND

The Miniature Pinscher Club
>Hon Secretary: Mr Alan Saxby
>39 Nethergate Stanington,
>Near Sheffield,
>South Yorkshire
>S66 DH
>ENGLAND

Snaffles Pet Furniture Ltd
>Unit 8,
>Mooracre,
>Marston Trading Estate,
>Frome,
>Somerset
>BA11 4 RL
>
>**Tel:** 01373 454682
>**Fax:** 01373 454291

Nylabone Ltd.
>The Spinney,
>Parklands,
>Forest Road,
>Waterlooville,
>PO7 6AR
>ENGLAND